About the Author

Mark Brooks lives in Wolverhampton and has been interested in writing since he was a kid, he used to spend the summer holidays writing. His mother is to thank for his interest in writing as she, from a young age, drummed into him the importance of literature. When he is not writing or daydreaming about the Princess, Mark works at a law firm.

Poems For A Princess

Mark Brooks

Poems For A Princess

Olympia Publishers

London

www.olympiapublishers.com

OLYMPIA PAPERBACK EDITION

ISBN: 978-1-84897-911-6

First Published in 2017

Olympia Publishers
60 Cannon Street
London
EC4N 6NP

Printed in Great Britain

Dedication

Poems for a Princess is dedicated to a very, very special girl –
"The Princess" - the most beautiful girl in the world!

Princess, I hope that when I give you a copy of this book and
'hopefully' you read it, that you will realise that you are the
girl, "The Princess", that inspired me to write this book. This
book is written especially for you.

Princess, I wish I had the confidence to tell you how I feel
about you, but I'm not very good at expressing my emotions
and feelings – I tend to bottle things up, maybe because I'm
scared of looking stupid or being rejected or what others think,
or a combination of all three and so this is my way of telling
you what I wish I could tell you in person,

Princess, this is for you. I just hope you like it.

All my love,

Mark.
xx

Acknowledgements

Firstly, I would like to thank my mum and dad. My late mum, for reading with me and helping me with my writing as a child, it's paid off! My first book published. Thanks, Mum, I know you're looking down on me and hopefully I'm doing you proud.

I would also like to thank all my friends and family for their loving support and encouragement.

A special thank you to Emma Beth Bailey for giving me the kick up the backside and telling me to "just go for it" and now look!

I also want to say thank you to all those who said I couldn't do it – you doubting me gave me even more determination to prove you wrong and do it.

A big thank you to all at Olympia Publishers for giving me this opportunity to reach you, the reading public.

Again, thank you to you, for buying and reading my book – I hope you enjoy it.

And last but definitely not least, a huge thank you to the inspiration behind the book, the reason I wrote the book – thank you to you, "The Princess", I hope the book tells you how I really feel about you.

FOREWORD

Hi, I'm Mark Brooks, or "Brooksie" to friends, of which, I now class you, and I thank you for purchasing my book. I hope you enjoy it.

This book is a collection of poems that I have written and my inspiration behind them is the most beautiful girl in the world (to me) - we'll call her the "Princess". I am not one for expressing my feelings or emotions verbally, I guess I find it hard, so I tend to write them down and they have come out in poetry form, I hope the "Princess" likes them too!

I have always enjoyed writing and being creative ever since I was a young boy. I think the imagination is a wonderful thing, you can be whoever and whatever you want. There are no barriers, only your imagination.

Again, I thank you for purchasing my book of poems dedicated to the "Princess". I hope you enjoy reading them as much as I have enjoyed writing them but to be honest, the words just seem to come easily being inspired by something, or in this case someone, you are passionate about.

Thank you and love and happiness to you all.

Mark "Brooksie" Brooks.

Xx

Contents

Hugs and Cuddles   17

Healing Princess   18

The Day I Met You   19

I Can't   21

The Long Game   22

Dressed To Impress   23

Jose's Not Special Anymore   24

I've Got The Love Bug!   26

Words   28

Cupid   29

Love Will Find A Way   30

If Only You Knew   32

I Knew I Was In Love When ...   33

If You Were A Song Title   35

If I Was A Song Title   36

Princess – See What I See...   38

Beautiful is She ...   40

Stevie's Right!   41

I Want To Be ...   43

I Want To Be The Princess's   45

Superhero   45

A Smile Is Worth More ...   47

I Wish Upon A Star   48

Little Star Make My Wish Come True   50

Princess To A Queen   52

I Promise   53

Princess - I Thee Worship.   55

The Princess Is Number 1   57

Top Of The Chart For My Heart   58

Let My Dream Come True.   59

Hugs and Cuddles

A Poem I put together about hugs and cuddles, sometimes we all need a hug and a cuddle because sometimes we all feel down, perhaps scared, worried or whatever and want a hug or a cuddle to feel better. In my opinion, we should do it more often without needing a reason. Go on, give somebody you care about a hug or a cuddle for no reason and make someone feel good, safe and secure, go on show them you love them.

Sometimes life is a struggle,
And you just need a cuddle,
Sometimes you just need to be held tight,
And told everything is going to be alright.
Sometimes you just want a hug,
You want to feel warm and snug,
In the bosom of the one you love.

Healing Princess

Again inspired by the beautiful Princess – whenever I am feeling down and low I just think about the Princess and she lifts my spirits.

Whenever I feel down,
Only one thing can turn a smile from a frown,
When I'm out of sorts,
I think happy thoughts,
When I'm sad,
Only one girl can make me glad,
When I'm in a state of depress,
I just think about the Princess,
And with that all my worries seem far away,
Thoughts of the Princess brighten my day,
And when my heads all a mess,
And in moments of darkness,
She is the light,
Thoughts of her tell me everything will be alright,
She gives me happy and pleasant dreams,
Yes, thoughts of the Princess tell me things are not as bad as it seems.

The Day I Met You

*This poem is inspired by the day that I first met the "Princess".
I remember "clocking" her and she took my breath away. The
"Princess" was the most beautiful girl I had seen – I know all
guys say that but it's true, she was the most beautiful girl I had
ever seen and to me she was a reflection of perfection. It is a
day I will never ever forget. What I remember most is looking
into her beautiful brown eyes and her beautiful, cute smile she
gave me.*

I thank God for the day we met,
Ever since, on you my heart has been set!
Meeting you, I have truly been blessed!
And now there's something I really have to confess.
Oh Princess,
That day I met you,
I knew, just knew,
I was falling in love with you,
There was nothing I could do!
Powerless,
My feelings - I was unable to suppress,
Right from the start,
You captured my heart,
I had been waiting all my life for a girl like you,
And I must say, I love the view.
You're a girl of natural beauty,

A little cutie,
A lady of elegance,
You personify excellence.
I remember being greeted by your radiant smile,
The wait to meet you was definitely worthwhile.
A voice of an Angel,
Yep over my heart you have a strangle.
Softly spoken,
Feelings of love inside me you've awoken.
You send my heart into a flutter,
You get me all in a fluster,
A simple sentence I cannot muster,
I try to speak but instead stutter,
It was love at first sight alright,
I think about you day and night,
You make every day bright,
Of my day you are the highlight,
You are amazing,
You, I am always praising,
Princess,
You're the best,
The day we met I will remember forever,
And forget it never.
Yes indeed, the day we met ...
Is the greatest yet.

I Can't

My next poem again dedicated to and with the "Princess" in mind. I can't turn my feelings for her off. I couldn't help falling for her. I guess it's true what they say - we can't help who we fall for and I fell hard for the "Princess".

Princess,
You I need to address,
This point I must stress,
I can't unlove you,
I can't help that for you my feelings just grew and grew,
I can't help that I want to be with you,
I can't help that for you there's nothing I wouldn't do,
I can't help that you're the reason I smile,
I can't help that you're the reason waking up in the
morning is worthwhile,
I can't help that you're the one I think about all the time,
I can't help but wish you were mine,
I can't help that you're the girl I dream of,
I can't help that with you I've fallen in love.

The Long Game

*This poem I knocked up in five minutes whilst at work one day
– I do actually do work at work – it was my lunch break! Again
this is about the "Princess" and playing "the long game" if I
want to win her heart. As the song goes – "Only fools rush in."*

I'm playing the long game,
With only one aim,
That is to win your heart,
It's all about being smart,
For a wise man once said;
Only fools rush in,
It's about planning ahead,
I'm only just about to begin,
They say good things come to those who wait,
Patience is a virtue,
And I want you!
So I better step up to the plate,
This will be a tough test,
I better be at my best,
To prove to you that I'm better than the rest!
It's going to be a fight,
But I'm ready to show you that I'm your Mr Right,
So let the game of chase begin,
I'm determined that your heart I will win.

Dressed To Impress

I'm dressed to impress,
The girl I like best,
When it comes to her,
There is no contest!
No one comes close to her,
No-one else can compare,
I can't help but stand and stare,
As she sits over there.
I look on from a distance,
She's a real sight of beauty,
A real life cutie,
I long for her to just give me a glance.
I'm stood there in my suit,
She's sat there looking cute!
Oh why does she not notice me?
Notice me - why doesn't she?
What I'd give for a chance ...
Maybe even a romance,
I'd settle for a date!
Oh why can't she be my fate?

Jose's Not Special Anymore

This poem again was a poem that I knocked up in five minutes at work one lunchtime. The inspiration behind this is obviously the "Princess" but the full story how this poem came about was that I heard someone mention Jose Mourinho's name and it came to me that he calls himself the "Special One" but I was thinking about the "Princess" at the time and it got me thinking that in my heart and my eyes and my mind that she is the "Special One" and hence this poem was created.

Jose, Jose
You're not special anymore
No way!
I'm making the call!
Your time has gone
There is only one special one!
It's not you,
There's nothing you can do!
It's not even me,
It's she!
The beauty,
The little dark haired cutie,
The princess,
For she is the very, very best!
To her, no-one can compare,

She beats all the rest,
Hands down, fair and square,
No-one come close,
To the girl I adore most!
She is the Princess!
The very, very best,
She is truly the special one
Sorry, Jose you just have to accept it son!

I've Got The Love Bug!

This poem I wrote to explain how the "Princess" makes me feel, I put the symptoms down to being in love and having the "Love Bug". I don't think there is any cure for this!

I can't believe this is happening to me!
It cannot be!
I've got this warm fuzzy feeling,
And it's even affecting my breathing!
My heart is racing,
I guess it's the love bug I'm facing!
For it's you I've fallen for,
It's love for sure!
I can't get you out of my head,
You've got me walking around half dead...
Because of you I cannot sleep or eat,
This love bug has me well and truly beat!
As I lay in my bed,
You're all that's running through my head,
I can't sleep,
Sometimes I weep,
Because all I think about is you!
What am I going to do?
There's no cure,
For this love bug for sure!

When I see you my heart aches,
In your presence I get the shakes,
I love you so much,
I long for your touch,
Maybe I should tell you how I feel?
Maybe only then can I start to heal!
I'm addicted, you're like a drug,
This damn love bug!

Words

This poem again I knocked up whilst thinking about the "Princess" and feeling frustrated with myself for not having the nerve to tell her how I feel about her or even what words I would use to tell her but then again I do find it easier to write down how I feel as opposed to expressing my feelings verbally.

Words, so many from which to choose,
So how is it so I can never find the right words to use?
To tell the Princess,
That I love best,
How I feel,
My feelings I want to reveal,
This isn't good for a supposed wordsmith!
Perhaps me being good with words is a myth?
They have to be perfect,
I cannot afford any defect,
They have to have meaning,
They have to be words said with feeling,
They have to be words of passion and love,
To show her that she is the girl I have always dreamed of,
They have to be words oh so true,
They have to say to her that I love you.
Words, so many from which to choose,
Difficult to know which to use.

Cupid

This is a poem I wrote about Cupid – I hope his arrow works for me and lands me the "Princess"! I hope Cupid doesn't miss!

Come on cupid,
Don't be stupid!
Get out your bow,
And fire your arrow!
So please take aim,
In this love game,
Your target for me...
Is she;
The Princess;
Whom I like best,
She's better than all the rest!
I believe she's my fate,
So cupid don't wait,
Don't hesitate,
Fire, GO!
Don't miss though!
Let your arrow hit,
And to her I will forever commit,
She's the girl I adore,
And love her forevermore ...
Will I,
Until the day I die.

Love Will Find A Way

This poem is a poem I wrote before work one day and the inspiration behind it was, well I'm not actually sure really but I heard somewhere the quote or someone say "True Love will find a way", it got me thinking about how I feel about the "Princess", and how I hope that this saying is true and that love will find a way – a way of bringing me and the "Princess" together. This poem reflects the hurdles that sometimes you have to overcome for love to prevail and if you truly love someone no amount of hurdles or obstacles will get in your way – I mean what's that saying? How does it go? Something like "Love conquers all". Oh I do hope so. I hope love finds a way for me and the "Princess" to be together.

Shakespeare once said the course of true love never did run
smoothly,
But for the Princess whom I love truly,
I will scratch, climb and claw my way,
To just get to her and say;
I love you,
For you there's nothing I won't do!
In this game called love one often has to overcome several
hurdles,
Love often has one running around in circles,
Often obstacles will be thrown in your way,

But me, I won't let it sway,
Hell, fire and brimstone couldn't keep me away,
Nothing will stop me,
From getting to my baby,
For I love her,
I will get there,
For I say,
True love will always find a way!

If Only You Knew

Again with the most beautiful girl (in my biased opinion) in mind The "Princess". If only I had the nerve to tell her how I really feel. If only she knew.

Princess,
This is an address,
If only you knew,
How I really feel about you,
If only you knew,
For you there is nothing I wouldn't do,
If only you knew the anguish I am going through,
If only you knew how desperately I want to reveal,
About you – how I really feel,
If only you knew how you make my heart melt,
If only you knew how I felt,
If only you knew how beautiful you are,
If only you knew how much I admire you from afar,
If only you knew how I think about you all the time,
If only you knew how I desperately wish you were mine,
If only you knew how I long to be your Mr Right,
If only you knew how I long to kiss you goodnight,
If only you knew how I'd love to hold you tight,
Yes, Princess, if only you knew,
How I really feel about you.

I Knew I Was In Love When ...

This is a poem about how I knew I had fallen in love with the "Princess" at first sight and how she made me feel which when putting the symptoms together, I didn't need to be a Doctor to diagnose I was in love with her.

I knew I was in love when I first saw you.
I knew I was in love when I first looked into your beautiful brown eyes.
I knew I was in love when you smiled at me and all I could feel was my smile bursting on my lips and the warmth that spread over my cheeks.
I knew I was in love when the butterflies in my stomach fluttered at the very thought of you.
I knew I was in love when my heart skipped a beat every time I saw you.
I knew I was in love when looking at you and smiling for no reason was the best thing I did in a day.
I knew I was in love when nothing else in the world mattered other than your company and the smile on your face.
I knew I was in love when seemingly every song on the radio made me think of you.
I knew I was in love when all those love songs that seem stupid suddenly made sense.
I knew I was in love when I had been humming songs

endlessly without even knowing.

I knew I was in love when you were the first thing I thought about when I woke and the last thing at night before I went to sleep.

I knew I was in love when time did not mean the hands of the ticking clock but the moments that I spent away from you.

If You Were A Song Title

This poem was inspired by some songs I heard on the radio whilst lying in bed awake and they made me think about the "Princess".

If you were a song title you'd be "Beautiful"
Because you are.
If you were a song title you'd be "Could you be the most
beautiful girl in the world"
Because you are the most beautiful girl in the world - no
could she be, Prince, she is!
If you were a song title you'd be "The wonder of you"
Because you are wonderful.
If you were a song title you'd be "Always on my mind"
Because you are.
If you were a song title you'd be "Queen of my heart"
Because you are the Queen of my heart.
If you were a song title you'd be "Can't help falling in love"
Because I can't.
If you were a song title you'd be "Take my breath away"
Because you do.
If you were a song title you'd be "Simply the best"
Because you are and "better than all the rest"
If you were a song title you'd be "Perfect"
Because you are Perfect.

If I Was A Song Title

This poem was also inspired by some songs I heard on the radio whilst lying awake with the Princess on my mind and these particular ones sum up my feelings for her.

If I was a song title, I'd be "Words" Because they're all I
have to try and win your heart.
If I was a song title, I'd be "A million love songs"
Well a million love poems for you, Princess.
If I was a song title, I'd be "Lonely days" Because they are
without you.
If I was a song title, I'd be "Someone like you"
Because I want you - someone like you in my life.
If I was a song title, I'd be "Can't help falling in love" I can't
when it comes to you!
If I was a song title, I'd be "Always on my mind" Because
you are always on my mind.
If I was a song title, I'd be "Amazed"
Because Princess, I am amazed by you.
If I was a song title I'd be "I want you, I need you, I love
you" Because I do, I do, I do!
If I was a song title, I'd be "Rescue me"
Come on Princess, rescue me from a life of loneliness.

If I was a song title, I'd be "I just can't help believing"
Because I believe dreams can come true if you believe and
pray hard enough and my dream is to be with you!
If I was a song title, I'd be "And I love you so" Because I do.
If I was a song title, I'd be "The greatest love of all"
Because the love I feel for you is the greatest love of all.
If I was a song title, I'd be "If I can dream" Because
everyone has a dream and my dream is to be with you.
If I was a song title, I'd be "Imagine"
Because I constantly imagine what life would be like with
you.
If I was a song title, I'd be "Teddy bear" Because I'd love to
be held tightly by you.
If I was a song title, I'd be "Stuck on you" Because I am.
If I was a song title, I'd be "Burning Love" Because that's
what I have inside for you.
If I was a song title I'd be "My first, my last, my everything"
Because you are everything to me.
If I was a song title, I'd be "My Girl" Because I wish you
were my girl.

Princess – See What I See…

My next poem again dedicated to and with the "Princess" in mind. I get the impression that the "Princess" doesn't realise how beautiful and amazing she is, but she can take it from me, she is beautiful and she is amazing, she is special.

Princess,
Don't be modest,
It's time to be honest,
See what I see,
I won't lie to thee,
You're a little cutie,
A real sweetie,
A heart of gold,
On my heart you have a stranglehold,
You're funny and clever,
The most beautiful girl ever,
You're beauty personified,
Though my true feelings for you I continue to hide,
You don't know how beautiful you are,
I admire you from afar,
I'm too afraid to tell you how I really feel,
But I promise you these feelings are real,
Go on Princess, look in the mirror and see what I see,
For what you'll see will be a reflection,

A reflection of absolute perfection,
That, I guarantee,
You are beautiful,
That is undisputable,
You're funny and bubbly,
Sweet and lovely,
You're amazing,
You, I could go on praising,
How special you are, I don't think you know,
But I'm telling you so,
You're the special one,
I worship the ground you walk on,
Princess, I'm in love with you,
It's true,
For you there's nothing I wouldn't do.

Beautiful is She ...

Beautiful is she who enters your life,
Beautiful is she who gets you through times of trouble and
strife.
Beautiful is she who makes your day worthwhile,
Beautiful is she who makes you smile.
Beautiful is she who brightens your day,
Beautiful is she who helps you find your way.
Beautiful is she who makes you her special thing,
Beautiful is she who makes your heart sing.
Beautiful is she who tells you everything will be fine,
Beautiful is she who says will you be mine.
Beautiful is she who gives you her heart,
Beautiful is she who says let's never part.
Beautiful is she who says take my hand,
Beautiful is she who says side by side we shall stand.
Beautiful is she who says there is nothing we can't overcome,
Beautiful is she who makes your heart beat like a drum.
Beautiful is she who makes you tick,
Beautiful is she who makes you lovesick.

Stevie's Right!

This poem was inspired by the Stevie Wonder song - "Isn't She Lovely" - the lyrics got me thinking about the "Princess" and so I got thinking and knocked this poem up. The song sums up the "Princess" pretty accurately in my biased opinion.

Stevie Wonder's right,
What a man of foresight!
It's almost as if you, he knew,
It's as if the song lyrics were written especially for you!
I think so anyway,
Here's what I have to say,
Listen Princess,
The lyrics describe you best!
Stevie sang "Isn't she lovely"
Princess, yes you are!
He'll have no arguments from me!
You are the most beautiful girl in the world - no-one is on a par,
Stevie sang "Isn't she wonderful"
Princess, yes you are - you make my life colourful!
Stevie sang "Isn't she Precious"
Yes, Princess, you are,
I admire you from afar,
You're luscious,

You leave me breathless,
You're gorgeous,
Princess,
I'm obsessed!
Stevie sang "Isn't she pretty"
Princess, yes you are - please let me love you ...
Oh please permit me,
For you there isn't anything I wouldn't do!
Stevie sang "Truly the Angel's best"
Yes, Princess, you are! Better than all the rest!
There is no contest!
So I conclude that Stevie you are a man of foresight,
About the Princess you are right,
For she is truly lovely, wonderful, precious, pretty and the
best!
To know her I am truly blessed,
Being her man is my quest,
But to achieve it, it's time I confessed,
For long enough I've kept my feelings suppressed,
It's about time they were expressed.

I Want To Be ...

Princess - something new
Especially for you;-
Titled - I want to be...
From me to thee.
I want to be your king
I want to be the one who gives you a ring
I want to be the one who makes you glad
I want to be the one who comforts you when you're sad
I want to be the one who holds you tight
I want to be the one that tells you everything is going to be
alright
I want to be the one that holds your hand
I want to be the one that is at your command
I want to be the one that wipes away your tears
I want to be the one to whisper sweet nothings in your ears
I want to be the sun in your sky
I want to be your guy
I want to be the one who of you is proud
I want to be the one who shouts I love you - loud
I want to be the one on whom you can rely on
I want to be your number one
I want to be the one to make you smile
I want to be the one that for you would walk a million mile
I want to be the one whom for you always has a tender kiss

I want to be the one that you miss
I want to be the one to be with you forever
I want to be the one you forget never
I want to be with thee
Oh please let me

I Want To Be The Princess's Superhero

Inspired yet again by the most gorgeous, beautiful and special girl in the whole world – the "Princess". I'd love to be her hero, hopefully one day my dream comes true.

Princess,
The girl I love best,
I want to be your superhero,
Your numero uno!
Spiderman envelopes baddies in his web from his glove,
And swinging from building to building,
Well Princess,
Who is the best,
I just want to wrap you in love!
It's love for you that I'm feeling.
Superman with his x-ray vision,
Princess,
Who is the best,
I see loving you forever as my mission!
Batman with his Bat Belt,
Driving his Batmobile,
Well Princess,
Whom I love best,
You are the girl that makes my heart melt,

Love for you is what I feel.
Incredible Hulk with his incredible strength,
Well Princess to make you happy I'd go to any length!
When you're sad I'd be your tower of strength!
Incredible Hulk – you wouldn't like him when he's mad,
But Princess, for you I'd do anything to make you glad.
Captain Marvel with his various superhuman powers,
To you Princess he bows and cowers,
Because Princess you are the only true Marvel,
But I'm bias, I love you, I'm not exactly impartial!
So Princess,
Forget the rest,
Let me be your hero,
Today, tomorrow,
Now and forever,
I love you, forget that never,
Princess,
You're the best,
Let me be your superhero.

A Smile Is Worth More ...

This poem was written about the "Princess's" beautiful smile.
One can never be down once you have seen her beautiful smile
– it's strange to describe but it sort of gives you a lift and you
forget your worries. Yep, she's amazing, her smile is beautiful
and uplifting.

To me, a smile is worth more than money,
I'm not being funny,
But one flash of a smile from my hunny,
The beautiful Princess,
Whose smile I love best,
Gives me a lift,
To me it's a beautiful gift,
I cherish every smile she gives me,
They give me so much glee,
A smile from her brightens up my day,
And all my problems somehow seem far away,
Her smile is beautiful,
It's undisputable,
I love her smile,
For one, the wait is worthwhile,
For her I would do anything to keep the smile on her
beautiful face,
Because in my heart she will always have a place,
So keep smiling Princess,
Yours is the best!

I Wish Upon A Star

This poem was inspired by as simple as it sounds, looking out the window one night and seeing the stars in the night sky, they brought back memories of that song "Catch a falling star and put it in your pocket, never let it fade away", and it got me thinking, I wonder if wishes do really come true and if you can really wish upon a star and anyway, to cut a long story short, I did, I wished upon a star and now, I don't know why, I do it every night before I go to bed, sounds stupid but I do it, not sure why, but I do it anyway.

Every night before I go to bed,
I say in my head,
As I look out of the window,
Up to that little bright glow,
Up in the dark night sky,
Way up high,
My wish upon that little star,
Up there away so far,
I don't wish to be a millionaire,
For money, I don't really care,
There is only one thing I wish for,
I wouldn't want anything more!
For if my wish came true,
I'll be jumping for joy and shouting woohoo!

For I wish for the Princess,
The girl I love best,
The girl I'd do anything for,
If I had her, how could I need anything more?
I wish for the Princess to come into my life,
I wish for the Princess and I to be man and wife,
I wish for the Princess and I to be together,
Forever and ever!
With the Princess in my life, I would be complete,
Life would taste so sweet,
So please little star,
Up there in the sky so far,
Let my wish come true,
Thank you.

Little Star Make My Wish Come True

Again, inspired by the beautiful Princess. If wishes and dreams really do come true I hope this is one of them! Sounds stupid but every night I really do wish upon a star for the Princess to complete me. She is amazing and special – if only she knew!

Little star,
Up there in the sky afar,
I look up to thee,
And beg you to grant a wish for me,
Little star burning bright,
Won't you make everything alright,
Oh little star I beg you,
Please make my wish come true,
I'm on my knees,
Please, please, please,
Grant my wish,
Just go swish,
And my dream will come true,
Thank you,
My wish I express,
Is to have the beautiful Princess,
I would need nothing more,
She is all I long for,
I would be complete,

And life would be so sweet,
So please little star,
Up in the sky so far,
Burning bright,
Make everything alright,
I beg you to make my wish come true,
Thank you.

Princess To A Queen

This poem is about my dream to make the "Princess" "My Queen", whom I would love, cherish, worship and do anything for.

Princess, oh beautiful Princess,
You I have to address,
For I have a dream,
Oh Princess, that is the very best,
It's time I confessed,
I want to make you my Queen!
How wonderful that dream does seem.
You're the Queen of my heart,
I knew from the very start
From the first day I met you,
I just knew,
Knew I was falling in love with you,
There was nothing to stop it I could do!
Oh Princess I have a dream,
A dream to make you my Queen!

I Promise

This is a poem of sort of commandments to the "Princess" that I will always obey.

I promise,
To the girl I pay homage,
Right from the start,
I will never break her heart.
I promise,
To the girl I pay homage,
Unto her I will be true,
There's nothing for her I wouldn't do.
I promise,
To the girl I pay homage,
That to her I will forever be faithful,
And tell her everyday she is beautiful.
I promise,
To the girl I pay homage,
That I will tell her I love her everyday,
And show her in every conceivable way.
I promise,
To the girl I pay homage,
That I would never let her down,
Because she's my Princess and she wears the crown.

I promise,
To the girl I pay homage,
That I will worship the ground she walks on,
Because she's the Princess and she's number one.
I promise,
To the girl I pay homage,
That I will love her forever,
And will let her down never.

Princess - I Thee Worship.

This Poem is inspired by the "Princess" whom I worship.

You are the girl I idolise,
You are the girl I worship.
I'll tell you no lies,
My heart - you have ownership.
To you I bow down,
You wear the crown!
You are the queen,
You girl, are my dream.
I worship the ground you walk on,
Princess you're number one,
My heart you have won!
Princess,
You're the best,
It's not even a contest!
To you no-one comes close!
For you, I love most.
You're worshipped like a Goddess,
I want to be your Adonis!
You - I would do anything for,
Of that you can be sure,
For you are the girl I adore,
I will love you forevermore,

My feelings for you I cannot ignore,
My heart belongs to you,
My soul too!
From the first moment I saw you,
I knew,
Knew I was falling in love with you,
To you I will be true,
Princess, I love you,
For you there is nothing I wouldn't do,
Princess, if you look into my eyes,
You will see that you girl are the one I idolise.

The Princess Is Number 1

Again this was inspired by the "Princess", whom in my biased opinion is the most beautiful girl in the world and definitely my number 1!

Princess, Princess, you're the very best,
Better than all the rest!
You're my number one!
My heart you've won.
You're top of the chart.
I knew from the start -
That you'd be the one to capture my heart.
To you no-one comes close,
To you who I love most.
No-one is even near,
My dear,
You're top of the league,
You fill me with intrigue,
You are gold,
On you, I'm sold,
You're the best in the world - it's true
I love you!
Princess, Princess - You've won,
You're my number one! You are indeed the special one!

Top Of The Chart For My Heart

My next poem again dedicated to "The Special One" (no not Mourinho) LOL (I already did a poem entitled "Jose's Not Special Anymore" explaining "The Princess" is "The Special One") but seriously this is dedicated to the "Princess", my number 1.

You're top of the chart,
When it comes to ownership of my heart,
Yes, there has been others stake a claim over the years,
They've been in line,
For this heart of mine,
But have no doubts, no fears,
This old heart is reserved for you,
The day I met you, I knew,
My heart has a hole in it where you should be,
So come on Princess, complete me!
I'm waiting,
So no hesitating,
This heart belongs to you,
To you this heart will be true,
So come with the key,
And you will see,
Inside there's something beautiful for you and me.

Let My Dream Come True.

Here's hoping my dream comes true and the "Princess" and I live happily ever after just like a fairy-tale.

If my dream came true,
I'd be with you,
If a Genie granted me three wishes,
I'd use just one, and that would be to make you my Mrs,
I'd give back the other two,
Cos' all I want is you,
You'd be all I'd hope for,
I wouldn't want anything more,
Please let my dream come true,
And let me be with you.